A Children's Book About

BREAKING PROMISES

Managing Editor: Ellen Klarberg
Copy Editor: Annette Gooch
Editorial Assistant: Lana Eberhard
Art Director: Jennifer Wiezel
Production Artist: Gail Miller
Illustration Designer: Bartholomew
Inking Artist: Barbara Baird
Coloring Artist: Berenice Happé Iriks
Lettering Artist: Linda Hanney
Typographer: Communication Graphics

A Children's Book About

BREAKING PROMISES

By Joy Berry

GROLIER ENTERPRISES CORP.

This book is about Sam.

Reading about Sam can help you understand and deal with **breaking promises.**

Have your friends ever failed to do
something they promised they would do?

Have your parents or other adults ever failed to do something they promised they would do?

People break a promise when they fail to do something they promised to do.

When someone breaks a promise:
- How do you feel?
- What do you think?
- What do you do?

When someone breaks a promise:
- You might feel disappointed, frustrated, and angry.
- You might think the person cannot be trusted.
- You might not believe the person any more.

It is important not to break the promises you make. People can trust you if you keep your promises.

People can depend on you when they can trust you. They know you will not let them down. They know you will be honest and not lie.

People will believe what you say if they can trust you. They will allow you to do more on your own.

You must show people you can be trusted
if you want them to trust you.

Show people you can be trusted. *Be where you say you will be.*

Show people you can be trusted. *Do what you say you will do.*

Show people you can be trusted. *Give what you say you will give.*

You must keep your promises if you want to be trusted.

It is important to treat people the way you want to be treated.

You should keep your promises if you want other people to keep theirs.